501 "*More*" Writers Useful Phrases

A further selection of 501 short, descriptive phrases, expressions and one liners to give *your* writing that extra punch.

QUENTIN COPE

I0427395

MECURIAN BOOKS

https://mecurianbooks.webnode.com

COPYRIGHT & DISCLAIMER

CONTENTS

:Introduction:

Appearance – Page 07
Conversation – Page 13
Fear – Page 19
Feelings – Page 25
Opinion – Page 31
Philosophical – Page 37
Senses – Page 43
Tenacity – Page 49
Time – Page 55
Viewpoints – Page 61

Introduction

If you are now reading '501 "*More*" Writers Useful Phrases', then you may already have in your collection the original ... '501 Writers Useful Phrases'. These little gems, contained in both editions, are not for the faint hearted. They are there to assist the enthusiastic writer and novelist who comes face to face with the odd case of 'writers block' ... the 'too much coffee ... brain not functioning' syndrome and the simply 'can't be arsed to write another word today' disease.

As we advised in the original '501 Writers Useful Phrases', you may be one of those fortunate and gifted writers who can simply knock the words out, get them down on paper, and after a morning recording a personal score of several thousand words, relax over a satisfying low calorie lunch ... and a large glass of even lower calorie Chardonnay. No fight with the wife, husband or kids involved ... just simple, straightforward ... bliss!

But hold on one goddamn minute! What if you are one of those poor, continuously striving writers who simply bleed to death over every sentence, knowing well what you want to write, but reluctantly unable to find that precise little phrase ... to exactly describe the moment. Good news ... this is the book for you!

Competent writing regularly requires reference to 'something' ... whatever that 'something' turns out to be. You are not a bad writer, simply because you cannot link a set of words together to express exactly how your character reacts or responds to a particular situation. You will become a good 'writer' by using the very best help and assistance out there in the big wide world of authoring, to get your work on track, correctly paced and seen to provide your characters with the kind of quality that sets your work apart.

With a Dictionary, Thesaurus and Scribblings all being put to good use, the experienced writer will collect over time a 'Golden Book' ...or 'Golden Computer File' ... that contains the condensed results of all the searching and researching for that short, concise 'Golden' sentence.

As we have said before, this second edition of the 'Writers Useful Phrases' is not the complete answer to a 'writer's prayer', but it is a great second line reference book of phrases you can use every day in your writing journey. So, what does 501 "More" Writers Useful Phrases contain?

It's simple really. If you have the first edition, this book is divided in to the same ten sections as the original version with each one containing 50 short phrases, quotes, expressions or complete sentences to fit a particular subject heading. The last section contains 51 entries, again making a total of 501 for this edition ... and here they are.

Appearance: This section contains some phrases and descriptive lines relating to how a character (looks) looked or (appears) appeared. It contains references to facial expression and the appearance of an individual or place.

Conversation: Here you will find a section of phrases, expressions and observations relating to how characters speak, how a conversation takes place or what has been learnt or surmised from a conversation.

Fear: This is a subject that has many parameters, but you will definitely find some phrases contained within this section to describe the kind of fear experienced by your character or the fear generated by a particular moment in time.

Feelings: This again is a broad subject that attempts to describe feelings in a mix of situations. Feelings of love, belief, disbelief, passion and reflection are provided to set the mood of a particular moment through the eyes of your character.

Opinion: This is a section covering the subject of opinion, which is simply that ... Opinion! Most of the phrases in this section relate to one individual's opinion of another ... or of a particular situation. One person's opinion of him/herself may differ from the opinion held by others.

Philosophical: There are a stack of useful quotes here covering a variety of subjects. This section is worth a regular visit as even if a particular phrase does not fit your pre-constructed scenario, there may be some that will trigger a useful line of thought.

Senses: This section provides a few useful lines relating to how a character senses situations or gains an impression of a scenario. Once again, this is a broad subject and it's impossible to summarize how the senses of a character lead him or her through a particular situation, but hopefully you will find some good links or triggers here.

Tenacity: This section describes situations and examples of tenacity taken or seen from your characters viewpoint, or that of others. One person's idea of tenaciousness will again differ greatly from another, but there are 50 very useful entries here to work with.

Time: Here are a few phrases and descriptions of 'time' as seen by a character or as seen in a particular and relative setting. Of course, we all know that 'Tempus Fugit'… but how do you describe it? There are entries here that will relate directly to time or to timelessness and there are 50 to choose from.

Viewpoints: Everyone has a different view of a similar situation and this section provides a broad listing of views and viewpoints relating to people and situations. This section is similar in subject matter to 'Appearance' but concentrates much more on a particular viewpoint relating to the appearance of an individual, group or scenario.

~~~~~~

Hopefully, you the reader … and more importantly, you the writer, will gain something more from this second writers new phrasebook in the series. It will make a great reference book and a significant addition to '501 Writers Useful Phrases' … not only at the initial manuscript stage in the production of your next epic novel, but at the tough edit stage where just one small adjustment can make all the difference.

The Author would like to thank you all for making '501 Writers Useful Phrases' so successful and simply wish you good luck in your search for perfection. Hopefully this new collection of 'little gems' will have played a part in the production of your next block buster.
Remember to … keep the faith.!!

Good Luck!

~~~~~~~~

Part 1:

Appearance

This section provides some phrases and descriptive lines relating to how a character (looks) looked or (appears) appeared or (disappears) disappeared. It contains references to facial expression and the appearance of an individual or place, along with thoughts and feelings in reference to ones appearance.

~~~~~~

01: When he first appeared in her life, she knew he would become dearer to her than night is to the thief

02: He was startled by eyes as luminous, bright and brown as waters of a woodland river

03: Then she was gone, disappeared - like the glow on a cloud at the close of day

04: He began to laugh with a sibilant sound, one that resembled the hiss of a serpent

05: He appeared to dance like a man attacked by a swarm of hornets

06: He lay still on the bed, like a warrior taking his rest

07: He saw disaster like a ghostly figure … following her as she moved away

08: She appeared frightened - like a child in the dark

09: He first appeared in her life at a confused and troublesome time

10: His initial appearance was as deafening and implacable to her as some elemental force

11: She was viewed by many as if charm upon charm was packed in her, like rose-leaves in a costly vase

12: It appeared that to all intents and purposes, he was bounded by the narrow fences of life

13: His face appeared as imperturbable as fate itself

14: He often wondered, in regard to his appearance - if he were drop-dead handsome, and every woman he met actually dropped dead, would he ever get tired of it?

15: She knew that although all men have eyes, when focused on a beautiful woman, few have the gift of penetration

16: As she studied her reflection, she knew she should be grateful to the mirror for revealing her appearance only

17: He knew the world to be governed more by appearance than reality, feeling it as necessary to 'seem to know something' as to actually know it

18: She gave him a glance that flitted like a bird

19: She saw only a quibbling mouth that snapped at verbal errors like a lizard catching flies

20: He appeared to be agitated like a storm-tossed ship

21: He appeared to have an indefinable resemblance to a goat

22: An undefined sadness seemed to have fallen about her like a slowly descending cloud

23: As she spoke, a tear like silver glistened in the corner of her eye

24: Her young eyes appeared to him as bright as day

25: The smile she softly used filled the silence like a well prepared speech

26: He looked to be as a man, who after following the plough all day, longs for supper and welcomes the sunset

27: The woman appeared as austere as a Roman matron

28: They were a couple who appeared … under close investigation, to be as close as oak and ivy

29: As she journeyed through the room, it was as if a door were suddenly left ajar into some world unseen before

30: She looked as innocent as a new laid egg

31: His expression turned as pale as any ghost

32: He looked at the extreme end of tension, like a well drawn bow

33: It appeared that dependency had dropped from her like a cast-off cloak

34: Emotions flashed across her face, like the sweep of sun-rent clouds over a quiet landscape

35: He suddenly became as fierce as a bear in defeat

36: His smile flashed with the brilliancy of a well-cut jewel

37: To her, he radiated vigor and abundance, like a happy child

38: She sat down in front of him, quaking like a jelly

39: He swayed in front of them, caught in the sudden grip of uncontrolled anger

40: He appeared to turn on her like a thunder-cloud

41: At very first sight, her beauty broke on them like some rare flower

42: Her hair was her jewel that hung down like summer twilight

43: Her lips had been likened to two budded roses

44: He looked with the bland, expressionless stare of an overgrown baby

45: She fluttered her eyes, her lashes like fans upon her cheek

46: She spoke to him, her voice rich and vibrant, like the middle notes of a vintage 'cello

47: Indifference appeared to fall from him like a loose garment

48: The sight of her hit him like a blast from the suddenly opened door of a furnace

49: He appeared to her like a mirage, vague and dimly seen at first

50: She hovered nearby like a fluttering leaf or falling flake of snow

~~~~~~~~~~
~~~~

Part 2:

Conversation

Here you will find a section of phrases and observations relating to how characters speak, how a conversation takes place, the philosophy of conversation or what has been learnt or surmised from a conversation.

~~~~~~

51: He told her the older he grew, the more he listened to people who don't talk much

52: She knew that most conversations are simply monologues delivered in the presence of a witness

53: He pondered on the speed of delivery, knowing the trouble with talking too fast is you may say something you haven't thought of yet

54: The real art of conversation is not only to say the right thing at the right time but to leave unsaid the wrong thing at the most tempting moment

55: She told him angrily that even a fish wouldn't get into trouble if he kept his mouth shut

56: He knew, before continuing the conversation, he would have to be careful of his thoughts, as they may become words at any moment

57: He sat there listening, knowing that silence is one of the hardest arguments to refute

58: Drawing on his fine command of language, he said nothing

59: He was a good communicator who never missed a good chance to shut up

60: He was told discretely that the difference between a smart man and a wise man is that a smart man knows what to say, a wise man knows whether or not to say it

61: After she left the room he revealed the trouble with her was she lacked the power of conversation ... but not the power of speech

62: She advised him to keep his words soft and tender because tomorrow he may have to eat them

63: He stopped the conversation short on the premise when arguing with a fool ... make sure he isn't doing the same thing

64: She spoke in a thin shrill, piercing voice like the cry of an expiring mouse

65: She interrupted the conversation with a voice soft and sweet as a familiar tune

66: His conversation was as agile as a leopard

67: The conversation changed from one subject to another, quick as the movement of some wild animal

68: The conversation started again as sudden and unexpected as a dislocated joint slipping back into place

69: The conversation collapsed like a depressed concertina

70: He spoke eloquently; every phrase delivered like the flash of a scimitar

71: He failed to speak with the fluidity of his thought

72: The unfortunate conversation played with grave questions as a cat plays with a mouse

73: Her face changed with each turn of the conversation, like a wheat-field under a summer breeze

74: Her voice cut through the conversation like a sharpened knife

75: Her words were delivered in a near hypnotic manner, sounding like wavelets on a summer shore

76: His voice rose up like a stream of rich distilled perfumes

77: He took the scatter gun approach, his talk like an incessant play of fireworks

78: He stood out in the debate like a moral lighthouse in the midst of a dark and troubled sea

79: She let words hang in the air like an eagle dallying with the wind

80: The words were as meaningless as the syllables of an unknown tongue

81: The conversation was filled with questions and answers sounding like a continuous popping of corks

82: After he spoke, she remained as quiet and expressionless as a nun's face

83: He was an orator possessed of sayings that stir the blood like the rallying sound of a trumpet

84: He spoke in sentences level and straight like an accurately hurled lance

85: She heard him like one in a dream

86: The discussion suddenly turned to silence, a silence that seemed heavy and dark; like a hovering storm cloud

87: Her voice came to him as soft vibrations of verbal melody

88: Sweet as music, she spoke; then retired from the conversation

89: Talking and thinking at the same time came to him like the open page of a monthly magazine

90: When he joined the conversation, the strange cold sense of aloofness that had numbed her senses suddenly gave way like snow melting in the spring

91: She knew he had spoken the whole truth, naked, cold, and fatal as a patriot's blade

92: The words kept ringing in his ears, like the tolling of a distant bell

93: Unutterable words pressed on his soul like a pent-up storm craving for a natural outlet

94: She captured his attention with words like honey melting from the comb

95: Her words fell on the conversation as soft as rain

96: His words soon became a copious torrent of pleasantry

97: His mournfully delivered words provided a distorted and pessimistic view of life

98: The conversation ended up as a nimble interchange of uninteresting gossip

99: When he finally spoke, his words offered nothing more than a profusion of compliments

100: The conversation ended with a sharp difference of opinion

~~~~~~~~~
~~~~

Part 3:

Fear

This is a subject that has many parameters, but you will definitely find some phrases contained within this section to describe the kind of fear experienced, or to be experienced by your character.

~~~~~~

101: She knew, in those first few seconds, she would have to decide if she *wanted* it more than she was *afraid* of it

102: He told her that fear is a darkroom where negatives develop

103: She accepted that many of her fears were tissue-paper-thin, and one single courageous step would carry her clear through them

104: Her fear was no more than the lengthened shadow of ignorance

105: This particular fear was his highest fence. Could he possibly climb it?

106: Fear made strangers of people who would be his friends

107: He felt that to conquer this fear would be the beginning of a new wisdom

109: He stated that every man, through fear, mugs his aspirations a dozen times a day

110: Fear is just your feelings asking for a hug

111: This person in front of her, who so feared life … was already three parts dead

112: Little did he know that the cave he feared to enter held the treasure he so desperately sought?

113: He told her, fear is the static that prevents me from hearing myself

114: He finally ran out of patience, telling her bluntly that fear is the cheapest room in the house and he would like to see her living in better conditions

115: If a man harbors any sort of fear, it percolates through all thinking, damaging his personality and making him the landlord to a ghost

116: He considered that fear is simply false evidence appearing to be real

117: He who fears to suffer, suffers from fear

118: He told her anything he'd ever done that ultimately was worthwhile... initially scared him to death

119: He knew immediately that to lead would be difficult when you're a follower of fear

120: He had accepted fear as a part of his life - specifically the fear of change. However, he went ahead despite the pounding in the heart that said -   turn back

121: Her fear was as fragile as a spider's web

122: He saw her fear, like a ghostly figure following her

123: He swayed back and forth in the sudden grip of fear

124: Her fear of him came and went like fireflies in the dusk

125: His fear, like his fortune melted away like snow in a quick thaw

126: The fears in his mind constantly murmured like a harp among the trees

127: The tingling fear kept his nerves thrilled like throbbing violins

128: The fear exploded on him like a knife-cut across the sinews of his not insignificant strength

129: His revenge overrode all his fears, descending perfect, sudden, like a curse from heaven

130: His whole fearful soul wavered and shook like a wind-swept leaf

131: Fear poured upon her like a trembling flood

132: It stung like a frozen lash, confirming her original fears

133: It was fear in confusion, like a whirling flood

134: The fear finally overtook him, like a caged lion shaking the bars of his prison

135: They ran in fear, like frightened porpoises pursued by a shoal of determined sharks

136: Conquering fear can be likened to a game in which the important part is to keep from laughing

137: He ran from the fearful sight, like a great express train, roaring, flashing, dashing head-long

138: His fear was replaced by weariness like a knight worn out by conflict

139: His fear followed him like a shadow permanently cast on a fair sunlit landscape

140: His fear talked to him like a voice from some unknown regions

141: His personal fears were laid out before him like two dead lovers who finally died true to each other

142: A fear like death itself, who rides upon a thought and makes his reckless way through temple, tower, and palace

143: A fear much worse than dining with a ghost

144: Like great black birds, the demons of fear haunt the woods

145: The fear appeared like phantoms gathered by her sick imagination

146: His fear of failure lay heavy upon him like the awful shadow of some unseen power

147: He stood in the middle, his fear steadying him like the boar encircled by hunters and hounds

148: The initial fright had turned to abject fear, lingering in his life like an unloved guest

149: The fear of loneliness struck him like a blow

150: In his immediate fear, he remained motionless as a plumb line

~~~~~~~~~
~~~~

Part 4:

Feelings

This is a broad subject that attempts to describe feelings in a mix of situations. Feelings of love, belief, disbelief, passion and reflection are described to set the mood of any particular moment through the eyes of your character.

~~~~~~

151: She knew the most beautiful make-up for a woman is passion; but cosmetics are so much easier to buy

152: She hated him with a passion so deep, sometimes it felt like love

153: He had taught her to be nice; so nice that now she was completely full of niceness ... she had no sense of right and wrong, no outrage, no passion

154: She could not understand the science that stated 'gravitation is not responsible for people falling in love'

155: She told him, there is no surprise to a man more magical than the surprise of being loved. It is God's finger on one man's shoulder

156: The feeling of infatuation is when you think he's as sexy as Robert Redford, as smart as Henry Kissinger, as noble as Ralph Nader, as funny as Woody Allen, and as athletic as Jimmy Conners. The feeling of love is when you realize he's as sexy as Woody Allen, as smart as Jimmy Connors, as funny as Ralph Nader, as athletic as Henry Kissinger and nothing like Robert Redford - but you'll take him anyway

157: Someone once said that love is only a dirty trick played on us to achieve continuation of the species

158: She came upon him, knowing that when love is not madness, it is not love

159: He asked one simple question. Do I feel in love with you because you're beautiful, or are you beautiful because I feel in love with you?

160: He expressed to her his love as an act of endless forgiveness

161: To his way of thinking, the art of feeling love... is largely the art of persistence

162: He displayed a feeling of lofty remoteness

163: She felt distressed at the obvious ghastly mixture of defiance and conceit

164: She felt it was a happy and compensating experience

165: They both felt they were witnessing a hideous orgy of massacre and outrage

166: She revealed to him what she hoped would be seen as a keenly receptive and intensely sensitive temperament

167: Her feelings took over the moment, breathing an almost exaggerated humility

168: He felt bound up with the impossibilities and absurdities of the situation

169: He felt the need for a brilliant display of ingenious argument

170: He observed her, triggering feelings of a fresh and unsuspected loveliness

171: His suppressed feelings would finally give vent to his indignation

172: He felt he was falling in to the well worn grooves of intellectual habit

173: She felt a growing sense of bewilderment and dismay

174: He felt he should harbor his misgivings in silence

175: She had the feeling he was about to pour bitter and biting ridicule on his discomfited opponents

176: She was already convinced his plea was to be irresistible

177: He felt it was an impartial and exacting judgment

178: She felt as if she was being impelled by strong conviction

179: She left him feeling in a position of undisputed supremacy

180: She was left in a whirlwind of mixed feelings and saddening memories

181: She felt in alliance with his steady clearness of intellect

182: His feelings would have to bow in deference to a unanimous sentiment

183: What feelings are they that one experiences in moments of the most imminent peril?

184: He felt incited by a lust for gain

185: She had more than a passing feeling he was the type of man who would be inspirited by approval and applause

186: She felt invested with a kind of partial authority

187: He felt his position had been laid down in a most unflinching and vigorous fashion

188: He felt un-attracted to lax theories and their corresponding practices

189: She had a feeling the whole situation was little less than scandalous

190: It was a feeling of mingled distrust and fear

191: She felt trapped by a mysterious and invincible darkness

192: He had a feeling her exterior was not so much polished as varnished

193: He felt himself to be on the sure ground of fact

194: He was sure it was one of the foreseen and inevitable results

195: He felt oppressed by some vague dread

196: He absent mindedly felt his scars to remind him that the past was indeed real

197: The worst feeling you'll ever feel is sitting

next to the person who means the world to you knowing that you mean nothing to them

198: He felt the success to be overshadowed by a fretful anxiety

199: She knew that despite her reserved inner feelings, she was passionately addicted to pleasure

200: He felt his patience to be under continual provocation

~~~~~~~~~
~~~~

Part 5:

Opinion

This is a section covering the subject of opinion, which is simply that ... Opinion! Most of the phrases in this section relate to one individual's opinion of another ... or of a particular situation.

~~~~~~

201: His opinion was that passion and prejudice governed the world camouflaged under the name of reason

202: If she was able to hold on to this opinion, then a dead leaf might reasonably demand to return to the tree

203: In his opinion, it was an impudent trick as hackneyed as conjuring rabbits out of a hat

204: It was his opinion that beauty maddens the soul like wine

205: The opinion was colored like a fairy tale

206: This opinion allowed dissatisfaction to settle on his mind like a darkening shadow

207: The opinion offered was so unique it flashed with the brilliancy of a well-cut jewel

208: The voicing of his opinion left a deep and brooding resentment

209: The opinion offered proved to be an attack of peculiar virulence and malevolence

210: This biased opinion appeared to have been blown about by every peculiar wind of doctrine

211: The opinion was thankfully cleansed of prejudice and self-interest

212: He had decided her statement was clothed with the witchery of fiction

213: Even under the cold gaze of curiosity it was still only an opinion

214: His opinion on the whole matter, disguised itself as chill, critical impartiality

215: His expressed opinions reflected his endlessly shifting moods

216: The opinion displayed the evanescent shades of her feelings

217: It was the opinion of many that every curve of her features seemed to express a fine but arrogant acrimony and a possibly harsh truculence

218: The opinion left them fatally and indissolubly united

219: It was only his opinion that generosity had been pushed to prudence

220: Opinionated haughtiness and arrogance were largely attributed to him

221: His initial positive opinion of her shattered as he felt the ironic rebound of her words

222: In his opinion, he found the necessary silence intolerably irksome

223: He submitted the required opinion to the others in brooding silence

224: General opinion agreed it was her stumbling ignorance which should seek the road of wisdom

225: With his opinion now fixed, it left his thoughts in clamoring confusion

226: In her opinion, he had yielded to the ingratiating mood of the day

227: The opinion was he could have been impervious to the lessons of experience

228: His opinion was colored by the mild and mellow maturity of age

229: Opinion was reflected in the indolently handsome eyes

230: The opinion he offered was due to his intense love of excitement and adventure

231: His opinion was wrong and into her eyes had come a hostile challenge

232: His various expressed opinions would lead to intimations of un-penetrated mysteries

233: The opinion had been heard; she sighed involuntarily

234: It was an opinion that involved a labyrinth of perplexities

235: An opinion is a thing most infinitely subtle

236: Some opinions can eventually be proved to be a simple but bitter disillusion

237: Her well articulated opinion seemed intolerably tragic

238: In his opinion, she had kiss-provoking lips

239: His opinion would be nursed by brooding thought

240: His well expressed opinion displayed occasional flashes of tenderness and love

241: His opinion was oddly disappointing and fickle

242: In his opinion, he was not paid to know why but to know how

243: The opinion was pertinent to the thread of the discussion

244: After listening to her opinion he was left with poignant doubts and misgivings

245: The rather unusual opinion was proclaimed with a joyous defiance

246: His opinion was subject to the red tape of officialdom

247: It was just an opinion, and respect forbade downright contradiction

248: It was an opinion that was limited by the rigid adherence to conventionalities

249: In everyone's opinion, she needed to be rudely reminded of life's serious issues

250: After listening to his opinion, she assented in precisely the right terms

Part 6:
Philosophical

There are a stack of useful quotes here covering a variety of subjects. This section is worth a regular visit as even if a particular phrase does not fit your pre-constructed scenario, there may be some that will trigger a useful line of thought.

~~~~~~

251: A house divided against its self can never stand

252: A man who is his own lawyer has a fool for a client

253: A woman needs a man like a fish needs a bicycle

254: Beware of power that corrupts as absolute power corrupts absolutely

255: Age cannot wither her, nor custom stale her infinite variety

256: To those who seek it, all publicity is good publicity

257: If you ask a stupid question, you're likely to receive a stupid answer

258: One of the frustrations in life is that toast always will fall buttered side down

259: A man with one watch knows what time it is; a man with two watches is never quite sure

260: Believe those who are seeking the truth, but always doubt those who tell you they've found it

261: Every good investigator knows there's more to the truth than just the facts

262: The obscure we see eventually but the completely obvious seemingly takes significantly longer

263: Losing an illusion often makes you wiser than finding a truth

264: Sometimes it's necessary to travel a long distance in order to journey back a short distance in the right way

265: If I tell you everything that is really nothing, and nothing of what is everything, do not be fooled by what I am saying; just listen carefully and try to hear what I'm not

266: You never know what's enough, until you know what's more than enough

267: Men are probably nearer the central truth in their superstitions than in their science

268: Think like a man of action, act like a man of thought

269: Don't miss the donut by looking through the hole

270: To learn something new, plan to take the path you took yesterday

271: The obstacle is really the path

272: Nothing in this world really belongs to us; at best we are borrowers, at worst we are thieves

273: Remember, if you chase two rabbits, you will be likely not to catch either one

274: It is better to know some of the questions than all of the answers

275: Only in the early morning light of life can we see the world without its shadows

276: Among creatures born into chaos, a majority will imagine an order, a minority will question the order, and the rest will be pronounced insane

277: What deep wounds ever closed without a scar?

278: Seeking the truth is not always the way to find it

279: We waste a lot of time running after people we could have caught by just standing still

280: You can't reason someone out of a position they didn't reason themselves into

281: He slept with faith and found a corpse in his arms on wakening

282: Tomorrow always comes, and today will never be yesterday

283: The weakest eyes are often fondest of the most glittering objects

284: You can see a lot simply by just looking

285: Reason and faith are both banks of the same river

286: Sometimes the questions are complicated but the answers are simple

287: He who depends on another man's table will often dine late

288: When the pain is great enough, you will let anyone be your doctor

289: One thousand people cannot undress an already naked man

290: When I die, I will not see myself die, at least for the first time

291: The human mind is inspired enough when it comes to inventing horrors; it's when it tries to invent a Heaven that it shows itself not fit for purpose

292: It's very strange when the life you never had flashes before your eyes

293: We become aware of the void only as we attempt to fill it

294: If you understand compound interest, you basically understand the universe

295: The opposite of a correct statement is a false statement. But the opposite of a profound truth may well be another profound truth

296: Sometimes an answer not yet 'blowin' in the wind' is stirring in the breeze

297: The hardest thing to hide is something that is not really there

298: Who is more foolish, the child afraid of the dark or the man afraid of the light?

299: There are some things you have to do by yourself, and yet you can't do them alone.

300: If a man will begin with certainties, he shall end in doubts, but if he will content to begin with doubts, he shall end in certainties

~~~~~~~~~
~~~~

Part 7:

Senses

This section provides a few useful lines relating to how a character senses situations or gains an impression of a scenario.

~~~~~~

301: He left behind a burning sense of shame and horror

302: She sensed a conscientious anxiety to do the right thing

303: They attacked his senses providing a constant source of surprise and delight

304: She sensed there would be little more than a crumb of consolation

305: She sensed that beneath his smooth exterior lay a cynical and selfish hedonist

306: He sensed an impending disaster of the first magnitude

307: It was a fastidious sense of fitness

308: It was a sense of hideous absurdity

309: He sensed he was entering a hotbed of disturbance

310: He displayed a keenly receptive and intensely sensitive temperament

311: She obtained a lively sense of what is dishonorable

312: His initial sense of negativity quickly became a lingering tinge of admiration

313: He had a sense this could turn out to be a mercenary marriage

314: She sensed there was a modicum of truth in the statement

315: She sensed his opening conversation to be a most unreasonable piece of impertinence

316: It had become a senseless passage of extraordinary daring

317: He had a sense he would be regarded simply as a pompous failure

318: It was a sense of deepening discouragement

319: He left behind him a sense of indescribable reverence

320: They sensed a sharp difference of opinion

321: He sensed a strong assumption of superiority

322: It was a sense of welcome release from besetting difficulties

323: She sensed he would always be observant and discriminating

324: Their senses were blended with courage and devotion

325: She sensed he was enjoying this brilliant display of ingenious argument

326: She sensed a calm strength and constancy in him

327: It would be conceded from a sense of justice

328: She sensed he was dangerously moving toward snobbery

329: He sensed she was dazzled by their novelty and brilliance

330: A sense of diffidence began to overwhelm him
331: There was a sense the argument was essentially one-sided and incomplete

332: He sensed an exact and resolute allegiance

333: She had a sense there would be frequently recurring forms of such awkwardness

334: His senses were overwhelmed by her fresh and unsuspected loveliness

335: His senses would tumble and stumble in helpless incapacity

336: He sensed a gratuitous and arbitrary meddling in the affairs of others

337: It began with a growing sense of bewilderment and dismay

338: She sensed a happy and gracious willingness

339: There was a sense amongst the onlookers his gestures and his gait were too untidy

340: She sensed his plea would turn out to be irresistible

341: He sensed from the interest being shown, he could almost allege it as a supreme example

342: He displayed an intense sensitiveness to injustice

343: He gave out a sense of having had intercourse with a more polished society

344: The sense was the involuntary thrill of a more than gratified vanity

345: His sense was this could be irrelevant to the main issue

346: There was a sense this could be a capital blunder

347: There was a sense this must be left as a matter of conjecture

348: She sensed the line of his argument ran counter to all established customs

349: He sensed it would be a fruitless and unthankful task

350: In one sense, this was little less than scandalous

Part 8:

Tenacity

This section describes situations and examples of tenacity, or lack of it, taken from your characters viewpoint, or that of others.

~~~~~~

351: The difference between tenacity and obstinacy is that one comes from a strong will, and the other from a strong won't

352: The tenacious road to success is dotted with many tempting parking places

353: When the world says, "Give up," tenacity whispers, "Just one more time"

354: If you pass all the pebbles in your path you will find you have eventually crossed the mountain.

355: When you come to the end of your rope, tie a knot and hang on

356: Consider the postage stamp: its usefulness rests in its ability to stick to one thing till it gets there

357: The greatest oak was once a little nut ... who simply held its ground

358: Perseverance is the hard work you do after you get tired of doing the hard work you already did

359: He who conquers is he who endures

360: You can't go through life quitting everything. If you're going to achieve anything, you've got to stick with something

361: The race is not always to the swift, but to those who keep on running

362: It's not that he is so smart; it's just that he stays with his problems longer than the others

363: He did not consider his perseverance as a long race; he considered it to be many short races ... one after another

364: The people who get on in this world are the people who get up and look for the circumstances they want, and, if they can't find them ... they make them

365: There is no telling how many miles a man will have to run while chasing a dream

366: Tenacity is a drop of rain making a hole in the stone not by violence but simply by falling … again and again

367: It's often the last key in the bunch that opens the lock

368: Saints are simply sinners who kept on going

369: Life is not about how fast you run or how high you climb … but how well you bounce

370: He knew he may not be there yet, but he is closer than he was yesterday

371: She knew that God's delays are not necessarily God's denials

372: Problems are not stop signs, they are guidelines

373: Tenacity shows not only in the ability to persist but the ability to start again

374: When your dreams turn to dust, it's time to get out the vacuum

375: Most people never run far enough on their first wind to find out they have a second

376: Tenacity lies in not letting the fear of the time it will take to accomplish something stand in the way of simply doing it

377: One door opens and as I go in I am faced with a hundred closed ones

378: Let tenacity be your engine and dedication your fuel

379: Success appears to be largely a matter of hanging on after all others have let go

380: Big shots are only little shots who keep shooting

381: Tenacity should always be considered as a pretty fair substitute for bravery

382: The history of the world is full of men who rose to leadership, by sheer force of self-confidence, bravery and tenacity

383: Luck is tenacity of purpose

384: Patience and tenacity of purpose are worth more than twice their weight of cleverness

385: The most difficult thing is the decision to act, the rest is merely tenacity

386: Men never cling to their dreams with such

tenacity as at the moment when they are losing faith in them

387: Diamonds are nothing more than chunks of coal that stuck to their jobs

388: You don`t judge a team by its record, but its heart and tenacity, two things you either have or you don`t have

389: Great works are performed not by strength but by perseverance

390: A champion is someone who gets up, even when he can't

391: His strength lies solely in his tenacity

392: If you are going through hell, you have to simply keep going

393: Ninety-nine times, the conclusion will be false. The hundredth time you will be right.

394: You should never give up on something you can't go a day without thinking about

395: Success is failure turned inside out

396: Character consists of what you do on the third and fourth tries

397: We must have a theme, a goal, a purpose

in our lives. If you don't know where you're aiming, you don't have a goal

398: If you're not failing every now and again, it's a sign you're not doing anything very innovative

399: The man who can drive himself further once the effort gets painful is the man who will win

400: There's no scarcity of opportunity to make a living doing something you love. There is only a scarcity of resolve to make it happen

~~~~~~~~~
~~~~

Part 9:

Time

Here are a few phrases and descriptions of 'time' as seen by a character or as seen in a particular and relative setting.

~~~~~~

401: As if you could kill time without injuring eternity

402: Time is passing, yet I'm the one who's doing all the moving

403: Men talk of killing time, while time quietly kills them

404: For disappearing acts, it's hard to beat what happens to the eight hours supposedly left after eight of sleep and eight of work

405: Time wastes our bodies and our wits, but we waste time, so we are quits

406: A good holiday is one spent among people whose notions of time are vaguer than yours

407: The flower you hold in your hands was born today and already it is as old as you

408: He who forces time is pushed back by time; he who yields to time finds time on his side

409: Time is like the wind; it lifts the light and leaves the heavy

410: There is one kind of robber at whom the law does not strike and who steals what is most precious to men … time

410: Time is a dressmaker specializing in alterations

411: How long a minute really is, depends on which side of the bathroom door you're on

412: Time is the corrector when our judgments err

413: Time is the coin of your life. It is the only coin you have, and only you can determine how it will be spent. Be careful lest you let other people spend it for you

414: Time heals what reason cannot

415: If you want work well done, select a busy man - the other kind has no time

416: The future is something which everyone reaches at the rate of sixty minutes an hour, whatever they do and whoever they are

417: The inertia hardest to overcome is that of perfectly good seconds

418: Time is the wisest counselor of all

419: There are whole years for which I hope I'll never be cross-examined, for I could not give an alibi

429: Time eventually brings an end to everything except time

430: Time is the only thief against which we can obtain no justice

431: Time is gift we want most, but... a gift we use worst

432: Time is the longest distance between two places

433: Time is but the stream I go a-fishing in

434: The present is simply a point just passed

435: It is essential to use time as a tool, not as a crutch

436: Now is the only time there is; therefore make your now wow, your minutes miracles, and your days pay

437: The time you enjoy wasting is not wasted time

438: A man who dares to waste one hour of life has not discovered the value of life

439: Whether it's the best of times or the worst of times, it's the only time we've got

440: Many of us spend half our time wishing for things we could have if we didn't spend half our time wishing

441: He had convinced her that time is like money, the less we have of it to spare the further we make it go

442: Until you value yourself, you will not value your time. Until you value your time, you will not do anything with it

443: We have only this moment, sparkling like a star in our hand - and melting like a snowflake

444: To get all there is out of living, we must employ our time wisely

445: Whatever you want to do, do it now! There are only so many tomorrows

446: In time and space, nothing is worth more than this day

447: Half our life is spent trying to find something to do with the time we have rushed through life trying to save

448: Time only seems to matter when it's running out

449: Time is what prevents everything from happening all at once

450: Time is but the stream I go a-fishing in now and again

Part 10:

Viewpoints

Everyone has a different view of a similar situation and this section provides a broad listing of views and viewpoints relating to people, situations and scenery.

~~~~~~

451: In his view, there existed a blank absence of interest or sympathy

452: To the gathering, it seemed to be a crystallized embodiment of the age

453: It was a distorted and pessimistic view of life

454: Viewed from any angle, this man had a great and many-sided personality

455: This viewpoint became a great source of confusion amongst them all

456: She viewed him with an icy indifference

457: He saw it as a brilliant display of ingenious argument

458: He seemed to be chastened and refined by the experience

459: He left them with the view that somewhere, there was a common ground of agreement

460: He knew he would be constrained by the sober exercise of judgment

461: She viewed it as an afternoon of painfully constrained behavior

462: They were expressions of unrestrained grief

463: During the conversation, he was viewed as being far off and incredibly remote

464: It was his viewpoint that fate had turned and twisted a thousand ways to abandon him in this place

465: To her mind, he was feigning signs of virtuous indignation

466: He observed glances and smiles of tacit contempt

467: He was haunted by blank misgivings

468: He reviewed the situation and then spoke with sledgehammer directness

469: He could almost allege it as a supreme example

470: From his point of view, the stranger had somewhat overshot the mark

471: He saw it as an impartial and exacting judgment

472: He felt impelled by a view supported by strong conviction

473: It was obviously said in deference to a unanimous sentiment

474: He entered the room in high good humor

475: In spite of plausible arguments he saw it as an attempt to bury his opinions

476: It seemed to him to be an inconceivable clumsiness of organization

477: He seemed to possess an inordinate greed and love of wealth

478: As he entered the room, he appeared invested with a partial authority

479: It was seen simply as a matter of conjecture

480: It was a view that would eventually become a link in the chain of reasoning

481: Looking at the matter by and large, the

conclusion was deemed as a lofty and distinguished simplicity

482: It looked as if he had been lulled into a sense of false satisfaction

483: He did not appear to be thinking straight and maddened by a jealous hate

484: What they had witnessed was seen to be the mere effects of negligence

485: Their common view was mingled with distrust and fear

486: The view was immediate and his worst suspicions were confirmed

487: He observed as she was moved to unaccustomed tears

488: He noted she was not averse to a little gossip

489: He took a view; obstacles that are difficult are not necessarily insuperable

490: He was obviously at variance with facts

491: He was looking at it from a high view standing on the sure ground of fact

492: She appeared to be on the edge of great irritability

493: Our views were diametrically opposed

494: He walked away displaying a painful and lamentable indifference

495: His viewpoint was genuinely parading an exception to prove a rule

496: Whatever he said, was peculiarly liable to misinterpretation

497: They appeared to be pelting one another with catchwords

498: He seemed to be working hard to predict the gloomiest of consequences

499: To all the listeners, these seemed nothing more than proud schemes for personal aggrandizement

500: There was a quickness to conceive but not the courage to execute

501: There was little doubt from his point of view she was regulated by the fixed rules of good-breeding

~~~~~~~~~
~~~~

THE END

www.quentincope.co.uk

MECURIAN BOOKS

https://mecurianbooks.webnode.com

www.ingramcontent.com/pod-product-compliance
Lightning Source LLC
Chambersburg PA
CBHW072255310526
45795CB00012B/1655